101 Things to Do in Greece

© 2017 101 Coolest Things

All rights reserved. No part of this publication may be reproduced, distributed, or transmitted in any form or by any means, including photocopying, recording, or other electronic or mechanical methods, without the prior written permission of the publisher, except in the case of brief quotations embodied in critical reviews and certain other noncommercial uses permitted by copyright law.

Introduction

So you're going to Greece, huh? You lucky lucky thing! You are sure in for a treat because Greece is truly one of the most magical countries on this planet. There's a mix of incredible ancient ruins, thrilling adventure activities, world-class festivals, and delicious food and drink that makes Greece one of the most enduringly popular tourist destinations on the face of the earth.

In this guide, we'll be giving you the low down on:
- the very best things to shove in your pie hole, whether that's traditional Greek street food or something fancier from a Michelin star restaurant in Athens
- the best shopping so that you can take a little piece of Greece back home with you, whether that's from a flea market in Athens or specialist jewellers
- incredible festivals, whether you want to party all night by the side of a river or watch an Ancient

Greek drama in an auditorium thousands of years old
- the most thrilling outdoor activities, such as kayaking around the Greek islands, or having a kite surfing adventure on the open water
- the coolest historical and cultural sights that you simply cannot afford to miss like the Acropolis and the Tree of Hippocrates
- where to party like someone from Greece and get down with the locals
- and tonnes more coolness besides!

Let's not waste any more time – here are the 101 coolest things not to miss in Greece!

1. Explore the Sand Dunes of Lemnos

Lemnos is a Greek Island in the Aegean Sea that you might not have heard about before. Because it's far from Athens, it's off the tourist trail, but that's all the more reason to visit in our opinion. Of all the attractions of Lemnos, there is one that really stands out, and you shouldn't depart before visiting the dramatic sand dunes on the island. The area is geographically a desert, and it is, in fact, the only desert in all of Europe.

2. Discover Ancient Treasure at the Acropolis Museum

While visiting the actual site of the Acropolis in Athens is, of course, something very rewarding, you won't see all of the archaeological items that have been found on the site itself. For that, you'll have to head to the Acropolis Museum, which contains around 4000 objects from the Greek Bronze Age to the Roman era, and Byzantine Greece. The museum has won numerous awards and accolades, and is considered to be one of the most impressive museums in the world.

(Dionysiou Areopagitou 15, Athens; www.theacropolismuseum.gr/en)

3. Visit a Stunning White Marble Stadium

The Panathenaic Stadium is the only stadium in the world that is built entirely from marble. This stadium is an important part of the ancient ruins in Athens, and dates way back to the 6th century BC. The stadium is particularly important because it has hosted many different Olympic games over the course of history, and the opening and closing ceremonies of the first modern Olympics in 1896 were hosted in the stadium. It was once again used as an Olympics venue in 2004.

(Leof. Vasileos Konstantinou, Athens)

4. Climb the Mountain of the Gods

If you are the kind of person who likes to get active and immerse yourself in nature while on holiday, an activity that's sure to get you breathless is a hike to the top of Mount Olympus, which stands tall at a height of 2918 metres, making it the tallest mountain in Greece. Luckily, there are quite a few different trails that can be taken up the mountain, so there should be something to suit everyone's fitness level. To start your trek, head to Prionia 18km up the mountain, which is where most of the trails begin.

5. Warm Your Insides With a Plate of Moussaka

Of all the foods in Greece, Moussaka is probably the most famous of them all, and so it would be one hundred shades of wrong if you were to leave the country without tucking into at least one plate of the good stuff. The dish is the epitome of comfort food, and it's essentially baked lamb mince and aubergine with a whipped yoghurt topping. It's the perfect thing for a chilly day, although it has to be said those are few and far between in Greece.

6. Catch an Open Air Movie in Athens

Athens is a city with a huge array of spellbinding attractions, but there are times when all you want to do is kick back with a great movie, right? Well, there is no better place to do so than at Cine Thission, which is largely considered to be one of the greatest outdoor cinemas in the world. The cinema has been open since the 1930s, and entertaining locals and tourists ever since. As well as a great programme of movies, the space also offers a view of the Acropolis and Parthenon.

(Apostolou Pavlou 7, Athens; http://cine-thisio.gr)

7. Explore the Sprawling Modiano Market

Thessaloniki, the second largest city in Greece is all too often overlooked, but it's well worth spending a few days there, particularly if you enjoy shopping. Modiano Market is one of the most impressive markets in the whole country, it dates back eighty years, and it sells a little bit of everything. Once inside, you will find handmade spice blends, preserved fruits and vegetables, coffee shops, bites to eat, and traditional handicrafts.

8. Enjoy the Festivities of Apokreas

When you think of carnival, your mind probably wanders to Brazil and other Latin American countries, but actually, carnival culture is also alive and well in Greece, except there it is called Apokreas. The festival ties in with Lent, and there are many different carnival celebrations all over the country, but they are particularly fun in Athens and Crete. At the centre of the celebrations are parades through the street. Everyone dances, sings, plays music, and has a great time.

9. Indulge an Inner Carnivore at The Butcher Shop

There is no shortage of great food to be had in Greece, and if you are a meat lover through and through, you are sure to be charmed by the magnificent Butcher Shop in Athens. This restaurant is situated next to the Gazi Gasworks arts centre and has tables that spill out on to the street. This is a traditional roast house that serves up slabs of meat, and we would recommend the free-pasture boar every single time.

(Persefonis 19, Athens)

10. Go Kite Surfing on Karpathos

Karpathos is a Greek island that has it all. Although it's stunningly beautiful, it is not overly touristy, and instead of finding people relaxing on the beach, you are more likely to find locals and foreigners enjoy the island's perfect conditions for adventure sports. Kite surfing is an activity that is popular here, and if you have an adventurous spirit, you are sure to love it. You basically get to ride the waves on a modified surfboard while holding on to a kite, which will propel you along the water at a great speed.

11. Purchase Something Special From Byzantino

As you reach the end of your trip in Greece, you will no doubt want to do a spot of shopping and purchase some souvenirs to remind you of your time in the country. Well, if you feel like indulging, we think there's no better place than Byzantino in Athens to make a purchase. The owners of this jewellery shop are obsessed by ancient Hellenic jewels and jewellery, and they aim to recreate pieces from classical Greece.

(120 Adrianou Street, The Plaka, Athens; www.byzantino.com)

12. Feel Ancient History at the National Archaeological Museum

If you are headed to Athens, you will almost certainly want to get to grips with the culture of Ancient Greece, and one of the best places to learn more is at the National Archaeological Museum of Athens, which contains artefacts from prehistory to late antiquity. This is one of the largest archaeological museums in the world, and some of the famous objects inside include the Igesous column, dating to the 5th century BC, and the Zeus statuette, dating to 440 BC.

(28is Oktovriou 44, Athens; www.namuseum.gr/wellcome-en.html)

13. Indulge in a Delicious Plate of Souvlaki

Souvlaki is one of the most iconic plates of food in Greece, and it's with good reason – it's simply very very delicious. If you have not tried souvlaki before, it is essentially meat, and sometimes vegetables, grilled on a skewer. It will most likely be served up alongside pita bread, pan fried potatoes, salad, and tzatziki sauce. The meat used is usually pork, but if you prefer chicken or lamb, you can find that as well.

14. Get Back to Nature in the National Gardens

There is so much culture and history to explore in Athens, that it can be all too easy to neglect the natural attractions that the city has to offer. If you are the kind of person who feels most at home when in nature, you will love to pass a tranquil morning in the National Gardens. Covering more than 15 hectares of space, the gardens contain more than 500 species of plants, as well as peacocks, turtles, and ducks.

(Amalias 1, Αμαλίας 1, Athens)

15. Climb to the Cave of Zeus on Naxos

Naxos is one of the greenest and most beautiful islands of Greece, but isn't so frequented by tourists. In our opinion, that's all the more reason to visit, and one of the highlights on the island has to be the Cave of Zeus. The cave is located on the mountain of Zeus at a height of around 600 metres, so it is a bit of a climb to get there. The story goes that Zeus spent his childhood years there and an eagle offered him a thunderbolt on top of the mountain.

16. Visit a Hill Where Paul the Apostle Spoke

Areopagus is a hilly area with rocks just northwest of the Acropolis. The reason why a rocky hill is so visited by tourists today is for a couple of reasons. Firstly, this is the place in Ancient Greece where the court was held for trying homicide cases. Secondly, Areopagus appears in the Bible as the place where Paul the Apostle delivered his famous speech, and it's thus an important pilgrimage site for Christians.

17. Get to Grips with Cycladic Art

When you think of ancient Greek history, you probably think of the Acropolis and the various temples that date back to around the 6th century BC. But actually, Greek culture goes back even further, and you can discover a totally different world of Cycladic art at the Goulandris Museum of Cycladic Art in Athens, which contains art works that extend way back to 3000 BC. Inside you'll find exceptionally well preserved figurines, marble slabs, vases, and weapons.

(Levidou 13, Kifisia; www.gnhm.gr/en)

18. Walk Through the Arch of Hadrian

The Arch of Hadrian, otherwise known as Hadrian's Gate, is an iconic monument in Athens that dates back to the Roman period. The really incredible thing about the structure is that the whole things is made out of marble. It is believed that the arch was constructed to signify the place where the old Athens and the new Athens meet. A selfie taken inside the arch is a thoroughly modern way of appreciating some of the country's Roman history.

(Leoforos Vasilisis Amalias, Athens)

19. Relax on a Black Sand Beach

Ask any local person on the island of Santorini which beach they think is the best of the island, and more often than not you will be directed to Cape Columbo Beach. Although the beach is very beautiful, it's also isolated, and at 12km from Fira, the island's capital, not that many tourists make it there. If you are a beach lover, we implore you to do so. There is black volcanic sand, and the beach is backed by dramatic cliffs.

20. Discover the Little Known Numismatic Museum

There are so many museums in Athens that sometimes the smaller museums, like the

Numismatic Museum of Athens, get overlooked, but if you do have a spare afternoon, it's well worth making the trip. The museum mainly contains a collection of coins, but there are also medals, stamps, dies, and masses, and the total collection contains more than 600,000 objects. The collection is organised well so that you can follow the history of coinage from ancient times to the present day.

(Panepistimiou 12, Athens; www.enma.gr/ht/exb_1stf1.htm)

21. Knock Back a Vanilla Submarine

There are so many hot days in Greece that you will almost certainly be looking for cooling treats right throughout the day. A treat like no other is the Vanilla Submarine, otherwise known as a Sugar Spoon. The basic idea is that you have a glass of water, you dip a spoon into vanilla fondant and then dip that into the water. You proceed to lick the fondant like a lollipop while sipping on the refreshing glass of sweetened water.

22. Have a Day of Learning at the Athens War Museum

When in Greece, there are plenty of opportunities to get to grips with Ancient Greek culture, but to understand a different aspect of the Greek culture, we recommend an afternoon at the Athens War Museum, the national museum dedicated to the Greek Armed Forces. If you are at all interested in military history, this is the place for you. You will find a helicopters, fighter jets, eighteenth century cannons, and huge amounts of artillery.

(http://www.warmuseum.gr/en/node/6)

23. Walk Through the Presidential Mansion Gardens

The Presidential Mansion in Athens is almost certainly the most important political building in the country, and is the official residence of the president of the Hellenic Republic. While this building is not open to the public, you are welcome to take a stroll around the six acres of the presidential mansion gardens. From there, you can take in the majesty of the presidential building, and spend some quality downtime in nature.

24. Be Totally Mesmerised by the Acropolis of Athens

Does the Acropolis even need an introduction? It is one of the most famous, beautiful, and beloved historic sights anywhere in the world, and a trip to Greece wouldn't be complete without seeing it at least once. This incredible complex of buildings, squares, temples, and monuments dates all the way back to the 5th century BC and contains the Parthenon, the Old Temple of Athena, the Odeon of Pericles, and many other important and stunning ancient structures.

25. Hike Through Samaria Gorge

While Greece might be best known for its ancient ruins, the country shouldn't be discounted by lovers of the outdoors who wish to find exciting adventures in nature. If you love nothing more than to strap on your hiking boots, the best place in Greece for a brisk hike is Samaria Gorge, a national park on the island of Crete. As the name would suggest, there is a gorge within the park, and it makes for a dramatic, but not overly physically demanding place for a brisk walk in the Greek sunshine.

26. Take in a Show at Technopolis

Technopolis is one of the most important cultural spaces in Greece. Every day of the week, there is something impressive happening, whether it's a new art exhibition, a shopping fair, a poetry recital, a panel discussion or a theatre performance. We give ourselves any excuse to go there, but the space is particularly great for performances, whether they are dance, music, or theatre. There are also plenty of places to grab a bite to eat and a drink on site.

(www.technopolis.bg/en)

27. Enjoy a Day at the Herakleidon Art Museum

Herakleidon is an art museum unlike any other, as its aim to is to showcase the intersection between art, philosophy, and mathematics. There are always new exhibitions inside the museum, but the permanent collection contains one of the biggest collection of MC Escher's work. Alongside the actual art work, you can find things like preliminary sketches, writings from the artists, and photographs so you gain a real insight into the artists' lives.

(Iraklidon 16, Athens)

28. Party All Night on the Island of Mykonos

Although Greece might be better known for its ancient ruins and the beaches on the islands, you should be in no doubt that the Greek people love to party, and you will find this out for yourself if you make it to the island of Mykonos. This island could be considered the party capital of the country, and there are bars and clubs to suit every kind of party person. We particularly enjoy Paradise, which is a club located right on the beach itself.

(Paradise Beach, Mikonos; www.paradiseclubmykonos.com)

29. Enjoy a Refreshing Plate of Dolmathakias

If you are visiting Greece in the summer months, like most people do, you probably won't feel like tucking into any food that is too hearty. Fortunately, one of the most beloved Greek foods, dolmathakias, are light and yet still full of flavour, and they can be found all over the country. These are essentially grape leaves that are stuffed with rice, pine nuts, and fresh herbs such as parsley and mint.

30. Peruse Ancient Artefacts at the Delphi Archaeological Museum

Discovery about Ancient Greece is not just limited to Athens, as there are important archaeological sites and archaeological museums to be found all over the country. One of the most impressive is certainly the

Delphi Archaeological Museum, which plays host to the many discoveries found at the panhellenic sanctuary of Delphi. Highlights from the collection include the torso of a nude male youth statue, bronze masks, bronze shields, figurines, and incredible mosaics.

31. Keep the Kids Happy at the Hellenic Children's Museum

With all of the complex ruins and incredible museums, you might think that Greece is the kind of holiday that won't be suitable for kids, but actually Greece makes for a very child friendly holiday destination, and you can even get them learning about ancient history on the trip if you take them to the Hellenic Children's Museum in Athens. In this museum, the vast majority of the exhibitions are interactive so that the kids can have fun while learning at the same time.

(Rigillis &Vasileos Georgiou B' Ave 17-19, Athens)

32. Hike From Milina to Lafkos

Greece is a country of immense natural beauty, and the best way to take all of that beauty in is with a brisk hike along the country roads of the country. One of our favourite hikes is a circular walk that will take you from the coastal town of Milina to Lafkos and back again in about two hours and a half. The walk is flat and even, and on the way, you will have a beautiful vista of the gulf, you can pop into local churches, and stroll through tree lined country roads.

33. Have the Best Easter Celebration of Your Life

The Greeks love to celebrate, and without a doubt, the most festive time of the year in Greece is Easter. If you manage to coincide your trip with the Easter celebrations, you will have the time of your life. There is no bad place to be in Greece during the Holy week. On Easter Saturday, you are likely to encounter drum processions and fireworks in the streets to mark the resurrection of Christ, and on Easter Sunday, when fasting comes to an end, it is common to eat spit roasted lamb.

34. Get Cultural at the Byzantine and Christian Museum

Athens is a museum city through and through, and one of our favourites has to be the Byzantine and Christian Museum. This museum opened in 1914, and now contains more than 25,000 objects, many of which are very sought after, from the 3rd century AD to the late Medieval era. Some of the most special objects in the museum include a 4th century marble statuette of Orpheus, Byzantine ceramic ware from the 9th century, and marble slabs with intricate carving and design work.

(Leoforos Vasilissis Sofias 22, Athens; www.byzantinemuseum.gr/en)

35. Tuck Into a Fried Octopus Ink Sack

Yes, you read correctly. We are not talking about fried octopus flesh, which you have probably tried before, but the fried ink sack of the octopus. The ink sacks are very carefully removed from the body so they don't pop, they are then boiled and deep fried. This dish is most commonly found on the island of Kalymnos. If you are a daredevil with new foods, this is definitely one for the bucket list.

36. Celebrate Greece's Seafaring Heritage at the Miaoulia Festival

As a country with many islands and surrounded by water, Greece has an established and strong seafaring heritage, and Miaoulia Festival on the island of Hydra, is a celebration of this part of the Greek culture. Hydra is typically a very peaceful island because no motor vehicles are allowed on land, but things get altogether more raucous at the time of the festival, which takes place every June. Something not to miss is the burning of the boats on the ocean.

37. Enjoy a Greek Veggie Favourite, Spanakopita

Although it is true that the Greeks do like their meat, there's also a decent selection of dishes for vegetarians visiting the country, and one of our favourites is called spanakopita. This is essentially a cheese and spinach pie, and it's every bit as delicious as it sounds. The pastry used is typically filo pastry, and this makes the pie really light and crisp, and something you'd be happy to eat on a sunny day in a traditional taverna.

38. Kayak on the Ionian Sea

Greece is a very beautiful country, but just as beautiful is the expanse of ocean that surrounds Greece, and the best way to experience all of the majesty of the Ionian Sea is by taking to the open waters. Our favourite spot for some morning sea kayaking is at Amvrakikos Bay. The water is a stunning turquoise colour, and if you are lucky you may even spot dolphins or sea turtles.

39. Explore Europe's Oldest City, Knossos

While in Greece, it's essential that you make some time to visit the island of Crete, which is possibly the most fascinating of all the Greek Islands. One of the ancient sites on Crete is Knossos, which was the home of the Ancient Minoan civilisation. This is the oldest known civilisation known in Europe, dating all the way back to the 19th century BC, and that makes Knossos Europe's oldest city. The Palace of Knossos is a must-see, but get there before 10am to beat both the crowds and the heat.

40. Enjoy Island Life on Elafonisi

Greece is a country with many beautiful islands, and if you want to get away from it all, and enjoy the very best of peaceful island life, it can be hard to know which one to pick for a perfect getaway. For our money, paradisiacal Elafonisi cannot be beaten. The island is just a stone's throw from Crete, but it altogether more wild and rugged. On the island there are sandy beaches, turquoise waters, and hardly ever another person in sight.

41. Tour the Lychnostatis Open Air Museum

If you are not the kind of person who like to stroll the aisles of stuffy museums when you are on holiday, you might just be tempted by the Lychnostatis Open Air Museum on the island of Crete, because there is nothing stuffy or boring about it. The museum contains many objects related to the ethnic culture and folk traditions of Crete. Once in the museum, you might be enchanted by a Greek dance performance, the chance to see wine being pressed, or to see traditional weaving in front of your eyes.

(www.lychnostatis.gr)

42. Eat a Plate of Feta Me Meli

Greece has no shortage of yummy food, and one of our favourite things to eat is Feta Me Meli. This is traditionally eaten as a starter, but we could eat them as a snack at any time of the day. The basic idea is that salty feta cheese is baked inside crispy filo pastry, which is then drenched in sweet honey. The interplay between salty and sweet, and crispy and soft is nothing short of exceptional. You'll be back for a second plate, we can guarantee it.

43. Watch a Show at the Fougaro Cultural Centre

If you are not so much of a big city person, and you are looking for somewhere that is quiet but still cultural outside of Athens, we always enjoy time spent in the small port town of Nafplio. There are lovely seaside restaurants, but if you make it to Nafplio, we can almost guarantee that you'll spend most of your time at the Fougaro Cultural Centre. Everything in the café and restaurant is delicious, but it's the evening shows that really stand out. If you want to be entertained, this is the place to be.

(Leof. Asklipiou 98, Nafplio; www.fougaro.gr)

44. Watch an Ancient Greek Drama at the Athens & Epidaurus Festival

The Athens & Epidaurus Festival is not some kind of three day affair, but lasts from May to October, and this makes it one of the most epic arts festivals anywhere in the world. Throughout the course of those six months, you can expect artistic talent from all over the world in Athens, so whether you are into contemporary dance or ceramics, there will be something that is up your alley. In the past, the festival has hosted Maria Callas, the Royal Danish Ballet, the New York Philharmonic, Luciano Pavarotti, and many other world class acts.

(http://greekfestival.gr/en)

45. Have a Cultural Afternoon at the Vorres Museum

If you think of yourself as something of a culture vulture, you absolutely can't miss out on the Vorres Museum, which spans six acres, and is dedicated to Greek folk and contemporary arts. While there is huge amounts of museum space dedicated to ancient art in Greece, there is not so much dedicated to contemporary arts, and the Vorres Museum makes for a refreshing change. Inside you will find many works from the 20th and 21st centuries, including video work, sculpture, installations, and paintings.

(Diadochou Konstantinou 1, Peania; www.vorresmuseum.gr)

46. Cycle on the Island of Kos

If you've seen just about as many ancient ruins as you can muster, and you want to take some time to enjoy the natural beauty of Greece, head straight for the island of Kos. This island has beautiful, rocky cliff faces, dandy beaches, and turquoise waters. If you really want to explore the island, you can do so easily on bike because the island is very flat and this makes it not too challenging as long as you aren't cycling in the midday sun. It's also the preferred method of transport for locals so the island is very bike friendly.

47. Be Stunned by the Parthenon

The Parthenon is often considered to be the most important building that still exists from classical Greece. This temple, dedicated to the goddess Athena, was completed in 438 BC, and its decorative sculptures are considered by many as the best examples of Greek art. Considering the age of the temple, it is quite incredible how much of this is still intact and how much you are able to see up close and in person, just as the Greek people would have done thousands of years ago.

48. Down Some Ouzo on Lesvos

The national drink of Greece is ouzo, a spirit that is made from a pressed combination of grapes and herbs such as aniseed, liquorice, wintergreen, and fennel. Without a doubt, the best ouzo can be found on the island of Lesvos, so there's where you should be headed if you enjoy a tipple. You can learn more about how the drink is made and its long history (it dates back to the 14th century) at the Barbayannis Ouzo Museum on the island, but the best education of all is knocking back a glass or two with the island's locals.
(www.barbayanni-ouzo.com)

49. Brush up Your Greek Language Skills

While it's true that many of the people in Greece speak good English, if you are sticking around in the country for a while, it can be a great idea to develop a few Greek language skills so that you can actually make pleasantries with the locals. One of the best places to do this is at the Athens Centre. And while you are there, you can also learn about Greek theatre, how to photograph Athens, and other cool subjects.

(http://athenscentre.gr)

50. Go Snorkelling on the Island of Milos

Milos is not one of the most talked about islands in Greece, but that makes it all the more appealing if you want a peaceful getaway. While Milos is a fantastic place for relaxed beach days and swimming in the sea, you can also get a little bit more adventurous with a spot of snorkelling. Because the water beneath you is crystal clear, you will be able to see all the beautiful, colourful fish swimming around in the same water as you.

51. Feel the Country's History at the Ancient Agora of Athens

There are numerous places of historical importance around Athens, but one of the most impressive of them all has to be the Agora of Athens, which would have been the very heart of Ancient Athens, where the population would converge for political, commercial, social, and administrative activity. The site dates way back to the 6th century, and includes a central court, a number of temples, and some monuments as well.

(www.agathe.gr/overview/the_archaeological_site.html)

52. Enjoy Drinks With a View at A For Athens

Yes, Athens is an incredible cultural city, but you can't go to museums in the night time, so this is the time when you can really enjoy what

Athens has to offer in terms of bars. A for Athens is a beautiful hotel in the historic part of the city, and the hotel has one of our favourite bars. This is not least because the bar is situated on top of the roof where you will have the most incredible view of the Acropolis while sipping on your glass of ouzo.
(http://aforathens.com)

53. Find Something Special at the Monastiraki Flea Market

Greece is such a vibrant country that you will no doubt want to take some things home with you that will always remind you of your trip. Well, if you love bargain hunting and searching for special items, you can't do much better than the Monastiraki Flea Market, which actually covers a whole neighbourhood, and is open every day of the week. Once there, you will find antiques, ceramics, handicrafts, textiles, and lots more goodness besides.

54. Enjoy a Filling Gyro After a Night Out

Greece does comfort food really well, and the perhaps the most comforting of them all is a gyro. If you've not sampled a gyro before, it is basically meat that is cooked on a vertical rotisserie, which is then wrapped in a flatbread and served with salad and tzatziki sauce. It is the perfect drunk food, and you can find it made from any kind of meat, so it doesn't matter whether you have a preference for chicken, lamb, pork, or even veal, you can find a gyro to suit you.

55. Have the Very Best Baklava of Your Life

If you were to name one Greek dessert, it would probably be baklava, and it's with good reason – baklava is sweet, sticky, and absolutely delicious. The dessert is essentially layers of filo pastry that are made sticky with drizzles of honey, and crunchy with nuts such as pistachios and walnuts. It may also be spiced with cinnamon and cloves. Great baklava can be found all over the country, but we really like them from Metropolitikon in central Athens.

56. Swim in the Clear Waters of Avlaki Beach

Sometimes, all you want from a holiday away is a picturesque view and some time swimming in the ocean. If that sounds like your personal paradise, you are sure to fall head over heels for beautiful Avlaki Beach, which is located on the island of Corfu. Because Avlaki is a pebbly beach, it doesn't attract the same number of tourists as sandy beaches on the island. But the water is crystal clear and it has even won awards for its cleanliness so it's the perfect place for a quiet dip in the ocean.

57. Take it All Off on Red Beach on Crete

Considering that Greece is a very religious and somewhat socially conservative country, you would probably be astounded by the number of nude beaches that can be found all over the Greek islands. If you feel like getting an all over tan, one of our favourite nude beaches is Red Beach on the island of Crete. The beach has its name because of its pink or rusty colour, but while you're there your attention might be taken by something other than the sand.

58. Get Folksy at the Museum of Greek Folk Art

Anyone who spends time in Athens is bound to be bowled away by the ancient ruins and museums dedicated to Ancient Greece, but more recent history can be somewhat neglected in Athens. But not if you head to the Museum of Greek Folk Art, which is dedicate to showcasing objects from the mid 17th century and onwards. Inside, you will find embroidery, weaving, costumes, folk paintings, stone carving, ceramics, metalwork, woodcarving, and more besides. There is also a library of more than 5000 books about folk art and folklore.

(Kidathineon 17, Athens; www.melt.gr/en)

59. Wave a Rainbow Flag at Athens Pride

Although Greece is a very religious country, this is not always reflected in the local politics, and while it has some way to go, Greece has been pretty accepting of LGBT people and their rights. Whether you happen to be gay or not, Athens Pride is a wonderful celebration that brings together the whole Greek LGBT community for a day of celebrations in the street. The culmination is always an epic parade with lots of colour, music, and dancing. It takes place each year in June.

(www.athenspride.com)

60. Discover the Karidaki Sweet

Although Greece might be better known for its savoury dishes, there are some truly wonderful sweets that can be found around the country as well, and one of the most unique has to be the karidaki. The karidaki is made from a whole, but unripe walnut, including the shell. The whole thing is soaked in water, carnation stalks, and lots of sugar so that the whole thing because sweet, sticky, and perfumed over time.

61. Enjoy a Day of Culture at the Benaki Museum

Athens is a city that has a phenomenal museum culture, but if you fancy taking a break from the many museums and sites that deal with local ancient history, you can experience something more contemporary at the Benaki Museum. The museum has been open since the 1930s and isn't concerned with just one topic. Inside the museum, you will find Chinese porcelain, contemporary Greek sculptures, Islamic art, and many other treasures besides.

(Koumpari 1, Athens; www.benaki.gr/index.asp?lang=en)

62. Sample Greek Wine at Brettos Bar

For a relaxed evening out in Athens, one of our favourite places has to be Brettos Bar. Located in the historic part of the city, this is

not just a bar but also a distillery, and a very popular place with locals for sinking back a few ouzos, brandy, and flavoured liqueurs. There is also an incredible selection of Greek wine behind the bar, so no matter your choice of tipple, you will find something that suits your palette (and gets you sloshed).
(Kidathineon 41, Athens; www.brettosplaka.com)

63. Look to the Skies for the August Moon Festival

While August is a blisteringly hot time to be in Greece, it's also a month full of celebrations and festivities, and it's worth planning a trip at this time of year if you can stand the heat. One of the most fun is the August Moon Festival. This occurs on the night of the full moon every year in August, and you will find live music performances is some of the most stunning locations around the country, such as the Acropolis and the Roman Agora.

64. Tuck Into an Authentic Greek Kebab

The kebab is a dish that is famous the world over but you haven't really had a kebab until you have gobbled one up in Greece. While you are in Athens, do not miss the opportunity to eat at Thanasis Kebab, which is widely considered by locals as the best place for kebabs in the whole country. They are the real deal and the prices are very reasonable, so we wouldn't be surprised if you return for seconds.

65. Venture up Mount Lycabettus at Twilight

If your idea of a great holiday is getting active and exploring somewhere on foot, Athens is a surprisingly great city for this. The tallest hill in Athens, Mount Lycabettus, stands tall at a height of 277 metres, and it's totally possible to strap on your hiking shoes and walk to the top. We think it's best to do this at twilight when the temperature is a little bit cooler, and the whole city takes on an astoundingly beautiful glow. If you want the view without the slog, you can also take the funicular to the top.

66. Purchase Some Souvenirs at Fira Market

If you are something of a shopaholic and you find yourself on the island of Santorini, you may wish to swap another beach day with some time shopping at Fira Market. Fira Market is without a doubt the number one shopping destination on the island, and it's the perfect place to purchase some special souvenirs. The most famous part of the market is "Gold Street" where you can find many jewellers selling designs in brilliant gold.

67. Get Musical at the Museum of Greek Folk Instruments

If you have any kind of musical streak, you might enjoy an afternoon spent at the Museum of Greek Folk Instruments. Here you can find more than 1000 instruments on display from the last 300 years. The instruments on display have been selected because of their decorative, aesthetic, musicological, and ethnological interest. And the building itself is also very impressive – a Greek mansion that dates back to the mid 19th century.

(Diogenous 3, Athens)

68. Explore Crete's Relationship to the Ocean

The island of Crete, totally surrounded by water, has an incredible nautical and seafaring heritage, and this is best explored at the Nautical Museum of Crete. On the first floor,

you can find recreations of ancient ship models. And on the second floor, you can find models of modern Greek navy ships, a missile boat, destroyers, and more. The museum is laid out chronologically so you can get a real sense of Crete's nautical history over time.
(Akti Kountourioti, Chania)

69. Indulge a Sweet Tooth with Halva

If you have something of a sweet tooth, you'll have no problem keeping it happy on a trip to Greece. One of our favourite desserts, and one that is very traditional, is called halva. Halva is a type of cake that is made using semolina flour instead of regular flour, and this makes the cake extremely moist. Olive oil and honey is drizzled right over the cake and it seeps into every part of the sponge so you are left with something gloriously sticky.

70. Have a Few Glasses at the Wine Festival of Dafnes

For the first two weeks of July, the village of Dafnes on the island of Crete transforms into a wine lover's paradise for the Wine Festival of Dafnes. Of course, the star of the show is lots of local wine, and you are welcome to sample plenty of it. But during the course of the festival, there are also culinary events and traditional performances and art events. It's a way of experiencing the beautiful island a bit differently.

71. Watch a Performance at the Annual Puppet Festival

Okay, so when you plan to visit Greece, the first thing that comes to mind not be to watch a puppet show. But if you are interested in the arts, the annual puppet festival on Hydra island, which takes place every summer is a must-visit. As well as local puppet artists, puppeteers from right around the globe are attracted to the festival to present their work. Companies that have previously performed at the festival include the Swedish Marionette Theatre and the Bulgarian State Puppet Theatre.

72. Gobble Down a Plate of Revithokeftedes

If you are vegetarian and worried about what you will and won't be able to eat in Greece, be sure to keep an eye open for revithokeftedes. Yes, the word will be a little tricky to say to your waiter, but it will all be worth it when crispy chickpea fritters arrive at your dinner table. You can think of these as a Greek version of falafel. They are crunchy on the outside and soft on the inside. Perfect with a side salad and some tzatziki for dipping.

73. Visit the Well Preserved Acropolis of Lindos

The ancient ruins of Greece are not only confined to the capital city, and some of the most impressive ruins can be found on Rhodes. The Acropolis of Lindos is beyond jaw dropping, an ancient city situated at the foot of a steep rock that used to be home to 17,000 people. At the acropolis, you can find a Hellenic stoa with 20 columns, the ruins of an ancient temple, and a clifftop enclosed by battlements. Take some water because there is no shade!

74. Drink Some Craft Beers at the Art Foundation

In the hot sun of Greece, there is nothing quite as appealing as a sipping on a bottle of ice cold beer. We reckon that the best place for a really flavourful glass of beer is at The Art Foundation in Athens. The Art Foundation would probably be considered an art space and café before it is a bar, but one of the really nice things about this venue is that it's so multi-functional. They have one of the best selections of craft beers from Greece behind their counter, and it's a comfortable place to relax for a couple of hours.

(Normanou 5, Athens;
http://theartfoundation.metamatic.gr)

75. Visit the Ruined Temple of Olympian

The Temple of Olympian Zeus is one of the most important ruins from Ancient Greece standing in Athens today. Although construction began in the 6th century BC, the temple wasn't completed until more than 600 years on. Alas, the temple was ravaged in the 3rd century and reduced to ruins, which have never been recovered. Although it exists in ruins, it's still an impressive sight to behold, and you can feel the expanse of Greek history when looking upon the temple.

76. Enjoy a Decadent Meal at Spondi

When you are on holiday, it's important to splurge once in a while and treat yourself to a decadent meal in a fancy restaurant, and it doesn't get much more decadent than a meal at Spondi in Athens. This restaurant has two Michelin stars and serves up contemporary Mediterranean food. The best way to experience a selection of culinary treats is by ordering the tasting menu, which is around 7 courses of deliciousness. Be sure to book a table well in advance, and ask for a place in their beautiful courtyard.

(www.spondi.gr)

77. Take in a Performance at the El Convento Del Arte

Once you have spent a long day sightseeing in Athens, you want to have a relaxing and fun evening once dusk falls, and for a fun night, we really love El Convento Del Arte. This is one of our favourite restaurants in town, and its décor of stained glass and velvet curtains make it feel really opulent. But the best thing about it is that there is some kind of entertainment every evening, whether it's in the form of Greek folk music or a spectacular dance show.
(Virginias Mpenaki 7, Athens; www.elconvento.gr)

78. Hike to the Top of Mount Taygetos

If you are really serious about hiking and want to take on an epic adventure while in Greece, we highly recommend a climb to the peak of Mount Taygetos in southern Greece. A hike up this mountain is particularly rewarding because you get to walk through dense forests, gorges, and ravines as you ascend. You should be aware that a hike to the top does take a couple of days so you shouldn't take this epic climb on unless you are a somewhat experienced mountaineer.

79. Chow Down on the Pies of Kythnos

While most Greek food can be found in all parts of the country, there is something in particular that you will have to travel to island of Kythnos for. The delicacy there is simply called the pie of Kythnos, and believe us when we say it's worth the journey. You can think of the pie as Kythnos as the Greek version of a cheesecake. A sweet cheese mixture is baked within a crispy filo pastry shell, and to say that it's decadent is a total understatement.

80. Visit the Theatre of Dionysus

The world of ancient Greece is well known for its magnificent theatres and stadiums, and one of the most impressive of them all has to be the Theatre of Dionysus. This theatre dates back to the 6th century BC, and at that time, more than 17,000 people could have been seated there to watch the performances. It is possible to visit the ancient theatre today, and the government is in the process of making it usable for future performances.

(Mitseon 25, Athens)

81. Climb the Santorini Volcano

The beautiful island of Santorini offers plenty of opportunities to get back to nature, and if you fancy something slightly more immersive that lying on the beach, we can wholeheartedly recommend a day spent hiking up the Santorini volcano. The highest peak is 565 metres in height, which makes this a doable day trek, although the climb can be steep at times. At the top, you will find a monastery that has been there since the 18th century.

82. Enjoy a Turkish Bath at the Bath House of the Winds

When you're on holiday, it's imperative that you take the time to pamper yourself and relax, and what could be more relaxing than an afternoon spent at Turkish Baths? The Bath House of the Winds in Athens is the only public bath house in all of the Greece, and it first opened its doors in the 17th century. You can take an audio tour of the hammam and then relax in the waters yourself.

83. Eat Lunch at a Seafood Taverna With a View

One of the most enjoyable things to do while in Greece is to sit down at a taverna on the coast, chow down on fresh seafood, and take in a killer view at the same time. There is no shortage of places that offer this around the country, but our favourite might just be To

Psaraki taverna in Vlychada on the coast of Santorini. Do not miss the grilled sardines stuffed with onion and parsley, and the Greek classic of fried calamari.

(Vlychada, Santorini, Vlichada; www.topsaraki.gr/joomla)

84. Get Back to Nature in the Valley of the Butterflies

If you manage to visit the stunning island of Rhodes, be sure to take some time out to visit the beyond magical Valley of the Butterflies. This nature reserve is found inland on the island, and makes a nice change from yet another beach day. As the name would suggest, the highlight of this nature reserve is the prevalence of the beautiful butterflies. The reserve is particularly bustling with beautiful butterflies of many species during May.

85. Shop Til You Drop on Voukourestiou Street

Voukourestiou Street is the street that you need to know about if you love nothing more than a spot of shopping on a lazy afternoon. This street in Greece's capital city is not exactly somewhere that you'll find an unbelievable bargain, but it is somewhere that you could find something extra special as this is the shopping street in Athens that really epitomises luxury. You'll find big brands like Dior and Louis Vuitton, but also independent designer boutiques that have more of a local flair.

86. Have an Artsy Day at the National Gallery

Athens is well known as being one of the most cultural cities in the world, and for an artsy day, you can't do any better than strolling through the aisles of the National Gallery. The museum was established in 1878, and since then the gallery has accumulated many important works of Greek and European art from the 14th to the 20th century. The space is expansive to say the least, and you'll find works from Rodin, Matisse, and Picasso to name just a few.

(Katechaki, Athens; www.nationalgallery.gr)

87. Pay a Visit to the Cretan Olive Oil Farm

Greek food is truly magnificent, but perhaps the best of all the grub in Greece is the olive oil. Whether drizzled on top of a Greek salad or on top of a kebab, the olive oil here has a quality like nowhere else in the world. And you can learn more about it by visiting the Cretan Olive Oil Farm on the island of Crete. On your visit to the farm, you can walk through the olive groves, see how the olives are pressed, and take home some delicious oil as well.

(Ag. Nikolaos; www.cretanoliveoilfarm.com)

88. Fly a Kite on the First Day of Lent

The Greeks are religious people, and it can be a great idea to coincide a trip to the country with religious holidays. Clean Monday, the first day of Lent, is a very pious day because this is the first day of Lent. But it's also cause for celebration, and something traditionally Greek that happens every year on Clean Monday is the flying of kites. Wherever you are in Greece, head outside and you will find colourful kites strewn throughout the sky.

89. Indulge a Sweet Tooth With Plenty of Tulumba

Do you have a sweet tooth? If so, you absolutely need to know about the tulumba, because desserts don't come much sweeter than this sticky and sugary treat. The basic idea of a tulumba is that it is fried dough, similar to a doughnut, that is then absolutely drenched in sweet syrup when it is still hot so that the sweet stickiness permeates all of the batter, and it is then eaten when it is cold. This is a treat that you can find being sold by street vendors.

90. Discover Sea Life at the Cretaquarium

As a country surrounded by water, Greece also has its fair share of sea life. If you'd rather stick to dry land, you can still discover all of Greece's amazing underwater life at the Cretaquarium, an aquarium on Crete, which is one of the largest and most impressive aquariums in Europe. There are more than 2500 species in the aquarium, so this is definitely the place to get acquainted with all of the beauty of the Mediterranean. Inside the tanks you'll find jellyfish, seahorses, sharks, octopi, and more.

(www.cretaquarium.gr/en)

91. Learn Something at the Museum of Byzantine Culture

If you make it to the second city of Greece, Thessaloniki, you absolutely have to spend an afternoon at the Museum of Byzantine Culture, which is one of the more impressive museums in the country. The museum opened in 1994 and has three permanent exhibitions: Early Christian Churches, Early Christian Cities and Dwellings, and From the Elysian Fields to Christian Paradise. Inside, you'll find jewellery, handicrafts, ceramics, glass objects, and more besides.

(Leof. Stratou 2, Thessaloniki; http://mbp.gr/en/home)

92. Go Fishing on Lake Volvi

Does your idea of a perfect holiday involve sitting on the edge of a lake in perfect silence while fishing on the calm waters? If so, be sure to plan a visit to Lake Volvi into your Greece itinerary. There are several fish species to be found in the lake so it's the ideal to spot to catch your own fish supper. Beyond the fish, there is also immense biodiversity on Lake Volvi with egrets, flamingos, herons, and storks as well.

93. Chow Down on Deep Fried Cheese

While Greek food might be slightly meat heavy, it's not all bad news for vegetarians visiting the country. If you see saganaki on any menu, don't hesitate to order it. Saganaki is deep fried cheese, and yes, that is every bit as good as it sounds. The Greek will typically choose a rubbery, salty cheese that will keep its shapes, such as halloumi. It is then served with nothing more than lemon wedges and a cold beer - yummy!

94. Visit the Triantafyllopoulos Winery

When you think about wine producing countries in Europe, France and Italy probably first come to mind, but actually, Greek also has a long heritage of producing wine, and on the island of Kos, there have been wineries since 500 BC. If you are a wine lover on the island, we highly recommend a trip to Triantafyllopoulos Winery. The family who run the winery will be happy to give you a tour, and it's a great place to purchase a couple of bottles to take home.

95. Visit the Tree of Hippocrates

Hippocrates, born in 460 BC, was a Greek physician, and one of the most renowned figures in the history of medicine globally. If you visit the island of Kos, you can visit the Tree of Hippocrates, and it's under this tree that Hippocrates taught his students medicine according to legend. The tree has become hollowed out over the years, and some branches are supported by scaffolding, but it's still an awesome place to muse on ancient history.

96. Dare to Try Kokoretsi

Greek food is nothing short of delicious. The cheese! The moussaka! The kebabs! But this is not to say that the country doesn't have its fair share of stranger foods, and one of these is called kokoretsi. Don't get us wrong, we think that kokoretsi is absolutely delicious, but it might take something of a food daredevil to try this dish, because it's essentially grilled lamb's innards. The meat includes intestines, lungs, heart, kidneys, and sweetbreads. Do you dare?

97. Venture Inside the Melissani Cave

When on the beautiful island of Kefalonia, a visit to the Melissani Cave is an absolute must. This fully developed cave was created by the dissolution of rocks, and is only accessible via water. A huge part of the cave's roof has fallen in, allowing light to shine into the cave in the most stunning way imaginable. This is the perfect morning excursion when you want a break from days spent on the beach.

98. Be Wowed by the Edessa Waterfalls

Who isn't wowed by the cascading waters of rushing waterfalls? Greece has more than a few of them, but our favourite has to be the Edessa Waterfalls. There are footpaths that lead to the viewpoint of the waterfalls, so you can take in the roaring water from a safe distance. Unfortunately, this waterfall is so powerful that it's not suitable for swimming, but feeling the spray of the water is relaxing enough on a hot day in Greece.

99. Party all Night at Venue in Athens

While it's true that the ancient ruins and the museums of Athens are very impressive, sometimes all you want to do is let your hair down and party. If that sounds like you, there is one club that is more famous than any other in Athens: Venue. The club has three epic stages, and it has attracted some of the best loved DJ talent from around the world, such as Sasha and DJ Tiesto. If you want to meet locals and party hard until the sun comes up, this is the place to be.

(Pireos 130, Athens; www.venue.com.gr)

100. Dance, Dance, Dance at the Annual River Party

When you think of the European festival circuit, Greece may not be the first country that comes to mind, but if you are a party person, you absolutely need to check out the annual River Party, which takes every August at the foot of Mount Grammos on the edge of the Aliakmonas River. Every year, around 50,000 people make it to the water's edge to listen to music acts, both Greek and international, playing their tunes across four different stages.

(http://people.gr/riverparty)

101. See Wild Turtles at Argostoli Bay

Argostoli is the capital of Kefalonia, but with 14,000 inhabitants, it's still a place where you can get away from it all and enjoy island life. There are many things to enjoy in the town but most people visit for one reason only, and that's the wild turtles that exist at Argostoli Bay. Loggerhead sea turtles are an endangered species, and these turtles make their way to the shore every morning. It's a very special sight to behold.

Before You Go…

Thanks for reading **101 Coolest Things to Do in Greece**. We hope that it makes your trip a memorable one!

Keep your eyes peeled on www.101coolestthings.com, and have a wonderful time in Greece.

Team 101 Coolest Things

Made in the USA
San Bernardino, CA
04 December 2017